HOW TO LIVE A HOLY LIFE

HOW TO LIVE A HOLY LIFE

DONALD GREY BARNHOUSE

Fleming H. Revell Company
Old Tappan, New Jersey

How To Live A Holy Life was first published under the title *God's Methods for Holy Living* (chapters 5–8) by William B. Eerdmans Publishing Company. Copyright 1951 by Donald Grey Barnhouse, Jr.

ISBN 0-8007-0768-0
Library of Congress Catalog Card Number 75-10900
Copyright © 1975 Fleming H. Revell Company
Printed in the United States of America

Τῷ ἀγαπῶντι ἡμᾶς καὶ λύσαντι
ἡμᾶς ἐκ τῶν ἁμαρτιῶν ἡμῶν
ἐν τῷ αἵματι αὐτοῦ.

CONTENTS

INTRODUCTION

Over the course of the years, any growing Christian reads many scores if not hundreds or thousands of books, some of which are helpful and others of which, quite frankly, are not. Only occasionally does one encounter a really exceptional book and know beyond any shadow of doubt that he or she has been blessed and changed by it. In my experience Donald Grey Barnhouse's little volume *God's Methods for Holy Living*, a part of which is reproduced here, has been such a book. Consequently, it is a joy to recommend a reprinting of these chapters to what I hope may be many thousands of other readers.

These chapters are versions of lectures originally delivered at the great Bible conference held each year at Keswick, England. Eight years after becoming the pastor of Tenth Presbyterian Church in Philadelphia, the church which I now serve, Donald Barnhouse was invited for the first time to speak from the Keswick platform; and the following year, in 1936, he was invited to speak each afternoon for a full week of meetings. The messages given on that occasion were published in England under the title, *God's Methods for Holy Living*, but they were not published in America, although about five thousand copies were imported. Two years later, in 1938, the young pastor was invited to speak again. On this occasion, he produced a second series of lectures that was published both in

England and America under the title, *Life by the Son.* This series went through several editions. At last both series were printed together under the original title, *God's Methods for Holy Living*, and were literally sent around the world.

This volume came into my hands during by boyhood and was the first work by Donald Barnhouse that I read seriously. I was just young in the faith at the time (as well as being young in years), but I was immediately struck with the value of these chapters for instruction in sound doctrine and in practical Christian living. In this form, the book began with the essentials of Christian life and growth: the new birth, assurance of salvation, justification, faith, prayer, and how to be cleansed from sin; and it contained an example of what it means to live a full day in close contact with the Lord. It ended with the power of Bible study, Christ's love, the hope of Christ's return, and the Holy Spirit as God's appointed means for growth and godly living. I can say that these lessons, simple as they were, literally became a part of me and thus guided and preserved me through many stages of my early Christian life.

As the second half of Donald Barnhouse's book is reproduced here under the new title, *How Grow in Holiness*, it is my prayer that these same lessons that so richly blessed me will also bless many others in this generation. The first half of the book is being produced under the new title, *Secrets for Successful Living.*

In each of his books, Donald Barnhouse inscribed as a dedication a text taken from the Book of Revelation. It read, "To him who loved us and freed us from our sins

by his own blood" (*see* Revelation 1:5). It is to that same
One, even the Lord Jesus Christ, and to His glory among
His own people that this reprinting is dedicated. May He
be glorified.

JAMES MONTGOMERY BOICE

Chapter 1

FINDING GOD'S WILL
IN HIS WORD

"Sanctify them through Thy truth: Thy Word is truth" (John 17:17).

ONE of the great purposes of the redemption that Jesus Christ provided for us was that here and now on this earth we might have life. It was not merely that we might be saved for the future, and thus come some day to dwell in Heaven, but that we might know today what it is to live Christ. John brings his Gospel to a conclusion, saying: "These things have I written that ye might believe that Jesus is the Christ, the Son of God." He does not stop there, but completes the thought: "And that believing ye might have life through His Name." So one of the principal purposes of faith is that we might know holiness in our lives today.

In thinking of some of the divine impulses to holy living, we shall look outward to the Word of God; backward to the cross; forward to the return of our Lord; and finally, within to the indwelling Spirit. In

all of these we shall find that we are looking upward to
our Lord Jesus Christ seated upon the throne making
intercession for us. In the midst of the high priestly
prayer of our Lord, we read: "Sanctify them through
Thy truth: Thy Word is truth."

Our English language is very rich in words, rich
beyond other European languages, because of the
Norman conquest. There came to England conquerors
who lived in the cities, while the Anglo-Saxons
dominated the country. Each had their own language,
and as the generations passed, they fused and gave us
both tongues in our present speech. Sir Walter Scott,
in the first pages of *Ivanhoe*, tells how "sheep in the
country became "mutton" in the town, and how
"oxen" became "beef," and how the "pigs" became
"pork," as they passed out of the hands of the Anglo-
Saxon farmers and into the hands of the Normans
in the towns. These double forms run all through our
language. "Fraternal" and "brotherly" have really no
difference of meaning, though they came from different
points of the compass with different peoples who in-
vaded this land. But this richness of speech is not
without its confusion in spiritual terms. Take for
example, the word "holy" and the word "saint."
There is no difference between them radically. "Holy"
has come to us from the Germanic, and "saint" has
come to us from the Latin, and has brought with it
related forms, one of which is "sanctify." This word
sounds more sweetly in our ears than one like "holify,"
so we have been spared that word. The meaning, however, becomes evident. We know that the suffix "ify"
added to a word means "to make it that," so, to
sanctify means to make saintly, or to make holy.

With that in mind, we look at our text and find that we may translate it: "Make them holy through Thy Word: Thy Word is truth." Every true child of God longs for the deepening of the Christian life. We have God-given desires for holiness. How important then that we should remember that the Lord Jesus, about to go to the cross, looked to the Father and said: "Make them holy through Thy Word: Thy Word is truth." It is an amazing thing, and we realize it more and more as we come to know the Word of God, that almost all that God does in this world today, He does by the Holy Spirit through the instrumentality of His Word. It follows that if we are to expect to secure blessings from God, we must receive them in the way that He has planned to give them to us. And though we may find holiness in many ways in the Bible, we shall not find it apart from the Bible.

We must recognize, therefore, that there are some ways in which holiness cannot come to us. We must not expect to find holiness merely through preaching, or listening to preaching. We have, all of us, met people who have been to so many Bible conferences and conventions that they can readily foretell a speaker's third point while he is still in the midst of the second! Yet such people frequently confess that they do not possess blessing in their own lives. They have listened without hearing. "Faith cometh by hearing; and hearing by the Word of God" (Rom. 10:17). Hearing is, of course, a Biblical term for obedience, that takes truth to the heart and submits self to its rule. A carnal Christian may listen to all the preaching available, but if there is no yielding to it, there will be no blessing.

Another truth we must realize is that God may use any part of His Word to bring the force of holiness into our lives. I have found in my own experience that God has used strange passages of Scripture to bring great blessings. I remember, for example, a study which I once made of the doctrine of Satan. As I found in the Word, God's revelation of what the Devil was, what he had been doing, what he wanted to do, and what he was never going to be able to do, the Lord used this knowledge to bring me one of the richest experiences of my Christian life.

Further, we must not expect to find holiness merely through prayer meetings. Prayer is vital, and the true Christian will find that the indwelling Holy Spirit draws the heart to God in prayer. Early in the morning, especially, we should find ourselves alone with God. Do not think, however, that by multiplying prayer meetings you are going to find the sanctifying power of God in your own life. I have found that prayer with the open Bible is the most effective. When you get down upon your knees and expect God to speak to you through that particular passage upon which you are meditating, you will find that He does speak. Many people make of prayer something that God never intended it to be. Prayer to them is a monologue instead of a dialogue. George Muller said that the most important part of prayer was the fifteen minutes after he had said "*Amen.*" People do not realize how they rush into the presence of God and how they rush out again. They treat God in a way they would never treat anyone of human renown. If by some chance you should be taken for an interview with the

King of England, what would you do? Would you walk in, and as you entered begin talking? "Oh, I am most delighted to be here, it is indeed a great honor. I have followed your career through all the years of your youth, and also followed you with my prayers. I have been greatly interested in all that you have done." Would you go on talking thus, telling him all about his kindness in receiving you, and then thank him for the honor without giving him the opportunity of opening his mouth?

You smile, yet is it not true that many people pray just like that? They come in at close of day, and say: "Now, let me see, I have been taught before going to bed at night to say my prayers." So they say: "Bless me and mine; give me this and give me that. Amen"; and then they go right back to what they were thinking about before they started the prayer. People may seek guidance in some such fashion, but there is a danger in guidance apart from the Word of God. There is a type of guidance current that is a sort of fashion with some people. From some of the experiences that they have desired to share with everybody, it would seem that their guidance has frequently been auto-suggestion instead of the direction of the Holy Spirit. If one seeks to have the mind brought to a state of blank quietness, there is danger that enemy voices shall speak counterfeits to the mind. Meditation with the Word is the safeguard that God has given us.

Then again, we must not expect to find that the life of holiness can be attained by any type of self-preparation. It is not by what some people have called "Tarrying Meetings," that the Holy Spirit is going to come upon us in power. Whenever you find anyone looking for an "it," there is always spiritual danger. It is to Him we must look. We must not be seeking an experience, we must be desiring Christ exalted in our lives. In Los Angeles a man became associated with a little cult in which all the devotees were looking for an experience which they called "the witness of the Spirit." This man went to a Christian who was deeply taught in the Word, and said: "Do you have the witness of the Spirit?" The Christian replied: "I have what the Word of God calls the witness of the Spirit." "Oh, but you don't understand," replied the man. "I went to tarrying meetings; night after night I waited and tarried, and I did not get 'it.' I went home and tarried further, and toward morning it was just as though a ball of fire came through the ceiling into my bosom, and burned and burned all the sin out of me. Did you ever have an experience like that?" The Christian who was taught in the Word, replied: "No, thank God, I never did. I would not know whether it came from God or the Devil." When a Christian begins to look for emotional experiences instead of looking for the quiet application of the Word to the heart by the Holy Spirit, he is on a wrong track, that can lead to nothing but deception, and can only delay the reality of blessing.

How many people have failed to understand the meaning of that word in the Acts, where the Lord told His disciples that they were to wait in Jerusalem for the promise of the Father. They were not to tarry in Jerusalem in order to become fit for the Holy Spirit, they were to wait for the calendar and nothing more, for the prophesied day had been clearly announced, and it was to be a day of God's grace, dependent upon nothing but His sovereign desire. If a man received an announcement that upon the King's Birthday he was to be made a peer of the realm, would he rush to London and say: "I must go and begin to feel like a peer; what can I do to make myself worthy to be a peer?" All he could do would be to reveal his ignorance. Rather would he wait quietly until the calendar brought the King's Birthday. Then his name would be published in the Honours List, and he would enter into his new position by the grace of the King. So it is with Pentecost. "When the day of Pentecost was fully come" the gift was given. It was not the day before nor the day after. It was fixed in God's calendar. It was announced as the Feast of Weeks in the 23rd chapter of Leviticus. Seven Sabbaths were to be counted; that is forty-nine days, and the morrow after the seventh Sabbath was the fiftieth day—Pentecost, which means literally the fiftieth day. It was on this fiftieth day the Spirit came, right on schedule, not because of any merit that was in those people, but because it was God's arrangement thus to work out His eternal plan in grace.

In addition to those negatives there are certain positive truths which are far more important. If we are to be made holy by the Word, it will be by appropriation of certain truths that are in the Word of God, and obedience to them.

First of all, I do not think that there is any possibility of real sanctification in any life until we possess the knowledge of what happened when we were saved.

I am not saying it is necessary for you to know when you were saved. One day I had a telephone call asking if I would call on an old gentleman who was nearing the end of his life. I went. It was in a simple home, and the wife said to me: "He has been listening to you on the radio, and he wanted very much that you should come and talk to him." He was an elderly Irishman, who had come over to America from Ulster, and, in the course of our conversation, I found he was trusting the Lord. After reading the Word and praying, we talked of other things. "How old are you, sir?" I asked. "I do not exactly know," he replied. "There were lots of children in our family, twelve or fourteen, I do not know how many, and an uncle brought me over to the States when I was seven or eight or ten, either in 1863 or 1864." I said: "Well, you may not know when your birthday is or how old you are, but you know you are alive, don't you?" "Oh, yes, I know I am alive!" So I say to Christians: "Do not get worried if you cannot say, 'I was born again on the 26th of July, or the 13th of February.' Do you know you are alive in Christ?" That is the first step, the foundation step for holiness, and no one can ever know it in the Christian life until he has entered into the knowledge of what happened when he was saved.

We were many years old physically before we knew we were alive. Certainly none of us at the age of one or thereabouts started to philosophize, and say: "I am a human being, I have life." We grow into such knowledge. One of the marks of the passing from childhood into manhood is the growth in the knowledge of all that occurred when we were born, and the knowledge of those processes by which we were brought into this world. In the matter of the new birth God lets us have this knowledge as early as we are willing to take it. It is thus that the Gospel is preached to the unsaved, but explained to the believer.

What happened when we were born again? We read in James: "Of His own will begat He us with the Word of truth." Here we find the Word is the means of the communication of divine life to us. Peter tells us we are born again, "not of corruptible seed, but of incorruptible, by the Word of God that liveth and abideth for ever" (1 Pet. 1:23). What is the Spirit telling us here? That our birth in Christ was the work of the Holy Spirit, who took the Word of God into the womb of the heart; there faith laid hold upon it, and from the contact of the incorruptible seed of the Word with our faith, there was created within us an absolutely new life. God did not take Jacob and begin to work on him to cut off one tendency and reform him in something else. God condemned Jacob and planted Israel within him. God did not take Simon and say: "We will have to polish him to make something of him." God said: "There is no good in Simon," and planted Peter right alongside the old nature. God did not take Saul of Tarsus and say: "There is a good bit there I could use." He said: "In the flesh there dwells no good thing," and put Paul within. Later Paul knew what had happened, admitted there was no good in himself, and said: "It is not I, but Christ that liveth in me" (Gal. 2:20). So the first stage in holiness is the knowledge that when we were saved, God the Holy Spirit came permanently to dwell within in an absolutely new creation.

That leads on to the second step, the assurance that we are saved. We should never say: "I hope to be, I am trying to be." Once in a while I ask some soul who is not quite clear about his spiritual state: "Have you been born again? Have you received Christ? Are you trusting the Lord?" And I get the answer: "Well, I hope I am saved. I am doing the best I can. I hope if I walk in the straight and narrow path for twenty years, I might be—possibly—perhaps." That is not the language of the New Testament, and there cannot be any true progress in the Christian life, any advancement in holiness until we have the absolute assurance that when God gave us life, He gave us eternal life, and that it is our present possession.

Why do you go down to the station for the ten o'clock train at ten instead of eleven? Because you believe the time-table of the railway company, that the train is to start at the hour announced. John, in the 5th chapter of his first epistle, says: "If we receive the witness of men, the witness of God is greater." Why would you believe the witness of man as to engagements and train schedules, and not believe God's Word that He has given you eternal life, and that that life is in His Son? So many people are timid about believing God, but He says we make Him a liar if we do not believe His record of life given in Christ.

There can never be any holiness in the Christian life, any reality that is firm and unshakable, if we doubt God. We must stand upon the Rock, knowing that what God has done He has well done and has done forever. Oh, that we might have in our testimony the language of the New Testament! Imagine Paul saying: "I hope I am saved; I am doing the best I can." He said: "I *know* whom I have believed, and am persuaded that He is able to keep that which I have committed unto Him against that day" (2 Tim. 1:12). "For I am persuaded that neither death, nor life, nor angels, nor principalities, nor powers, nor things present, nor things to come, nor height, nor depth, nor any other creature, shall be able to separate us from the love of God which is in Christ Jesus our Lord" (Rom. 8:38, 39).

What about John? John says: "These things have I written to you that believe in the Name of the Son of God, that ye may know that ye have eternal life" (1 John 5:13). He knew he had it. He was not going around saying: "I trust, if I do not fall away, that finally I shall be saved." He knew that God had given him His Son, and that in the Son he had eternal life. Peter says: "We are redeemed, not with corruptible things such as silver and gold, but with the precious blood of Christ" (1 Peter 1:18, 19). You may say: "That is all right for Peter and John and Paul, those giants in the faith, but what about some of the little ones?" Well, let us refer to Jude. He only wrote twenty-five verses, but this is one of them: "Now unto Him who is able to keep you from falling, and to present you faultless before the presence of His glory with exceeding joy" (v. 24).

These two truths, a knowledge of what happened when we were saved, and an assurance that it has

happened in our own lives, are prerequisites to any
further growth in the Word of God, and in holiness.
When I use the word "prerequisite," I do so that we
should understand it. You could not study Astronomy
if you had not completed certain preliminary studies.
Arithmetic is a prerequisite to Algebra; Algebra is a
prerequisite to Geometry; and Geometry is a prerequisite to Astronomy. You take these things in order,
and no one will be able to study the parabolic curves,
and the movements of the stars through space, who
does not know the multiplication table. You need not
expect in your Christian life to have the joyous over-
flow that some people know, unless you have passed
through the rudimentary course of prerequisites in
the Word of God. There must be the knowledge of
what happened when you were saved, and the assurance that it has happened to you. Then you can move
on to higher things.

A third step towards holiness is the Bible revelation
of the will of God. As we study the Word we find out
some of the things that reveal His will, and we learn
then to do them. Some people think they have done
quite enough for the Lord if they keep a nodding
acquaintance with the ten commandments. So far as
doing anything for the Lord from pure love, they know
nothing about it at all. But when we read carefully
the Word of God we find certain revelations of His
desires, and learn how we may be well pleasing in His
sight.

There was a simple man in the Western part of the
United States who was saved, and they asked him what
difference it had made in his life. He said: "I am a

butcher, and since I have been saved I have stopped weighing my thumb. I sold that thumb for the price of beef hundreds of times. Then I found in the Word of God that 'a false balance is an abomination to the Lord.' " In reading the Word that man had discovered a practical point about the will of the Father, and he was growing in the Spirit by applying that Word to his scales. Thus he was beginning to know a little more of sanctification.

People say: "How am I to know the will of God?" I can tell you from my own personal experience that ninety per cent of knowing the will of God consists in being willing to do it even before you know it. We must realize that in our Christian life God is desiring to be loved by us, wanting us to seek out His will, to know it and do it. If there is not real love, there cannot be any desire to do His will.

At the Keswick Convention a gentleman came to me on the street, pulled out a photograph, and said: "Do you know these two young people?" I had received a photograph of the same people a few days before. A young woman who found Christ in my church in Philadelphia went out to China as a nurse under the China Inland Mission. A young man saved in England went out to the same Mission in China and met the young lady. She wrote me a letter, three pages of it, telling me about Henry, but forgot to mention his last name. She said his pastor would be at Keswick, and he would come and see me. So his pastor came to me and said: "My Henry wrote me three pages about Helen, but forgot to tell me her last name." Now you know how it is when young people are that way, they like to do things that are well pleasing to the other.

A young man learns just by chance that his Helen likes violets better than roses, so he goes to a florist and says: "I want some violets." The shop assistant says: "I am very sorry, sir, we do not have any violets; won't you take some of these roses?" The young man says: "No, thank you," and walks twelve blocks to another shop, and he considers his twelve blocks well walked if he can find some violets. Why? Just so that when he gives his Helen the violets, she will say: "Oh, Henry, you knew I liked violets better than roses!"

There is a spiritual lesson in that. Have you ever really tried to find out what God wants? Tried to "surprise" His will? To say: "Lord, I have sought diligently to know what pleased Thee best, and in my life I have sought to bring forth just this fruit because Thy Word reveals principles which show that that is well pleasing unto Thee?" Thus we apprehend our Lord's will in matters which are not specifically mentioned in the Word. The Bible is not a set of rules, but a book of divine principles. As we yield to those we have learned, He reveals His will still further.

It is most important, however, that we be willing to do His will as soon as we know it; even before we know it. We learn a great deal from our children. A few months ago I walked out of our dining room with Miss Twelve-year-old beside me, and went to my study. A certain matter was being discussed. "Daddy, what do you want me to do?" I gave her a definite answer. She began to argue, and went on at a great rate. I sat writing as though I had not heard her. She was silent for a moment, and then began all over again, telling me why that which I had expressed as my will was wrong, and why it should be something else. After the child had said this about three times, her mother came into the room, and asked: "Why don't you come?" and the child said: "I am waiting to find out what Daddy wants me to do." I said to her: "Wait a minute, my dear, whatever else you may be doing, you are not waiting to find out what I want you to do. I told you what I wanted you to do the moment I came into the room. What you are waiting for is to see if you cannot get me to change my mind, and you cannot!"

Frequently you find someone who says: "I am earnestly seeking the will of God," when in reality they are seeking to justify their failure to do what they know God wants them to do. A young student in a theological seminary said that he was earnestly seeking the will of God as to whether or not he should marry a young lady who was not saved. Now the Word of God says: "Be not unequally yoked together with unbelievers, for what fellowship hath righteousness with unrighteousness?" (2 Cor. 6:14). Like the little girl, he continued quibbling with God to find out His will, when that will was revealed definitely and unchangeably in His Word.

If we are going to grow in holiness, we are going to come with a willingness to do His will and a diligence to study to find out what that will is. Not only does the Word of God give us this knowledge of what happens when we are saved, the assurance that we are saved, and the revelation of God's will in every phase of life, but it gives us something far more, it gives us a

knowledge of His whole plan. We learn the line of His
march in history, we learn enough of His present and
future plans to set our minds at rest. We are satisfied
when we know the Word of God. We are not troubled
by the rumors of rearmament, and not troubled by
the disquieting news that fills the press from day to
day, because we have been to the Word of God. We
know His plan. We are not worried about the latest
theories of the intellectuals who attack the Bible.
Young people who are concerned because of some of
the things that are being taught in our schools will
find all the difficulties disappear when they come to
the Word of God and learn His plan.

Suppose I go out one evening and see a group of
men standing upon a mound under a summer sky,
looking up to the stars, and I say: "What are you
doing?" They say: "We are astronomers, we are
studying the stars." "What, out here on a mound?"
"Yes, here we have a broad sweep, we can see the
whole horizon." I say: "Come with me into this
little house and apply your eyes to this little one-inch
eyepiece." They say: "Oh, no; we could not have the
narrow restrictions that you would impose upon us.
Give us this broad, fine mountain top." Yet we know
they could learn more in one moment by taking the
restrictive eyepiece of a telescope than they could
learn in a hundred years out on their broad mountain
top.

So it is with the Word of God. Men stand today
and say: "Look at the eminence to which we have
raised ourselves. We look backwards into history and
can see as far as the protoplasm in the primordial

ooze." We bring them to God's Word and show them even further: "In the beginning was the Word, and the Word was with God, and the Word was God, the same was in the beginning with God. All things were made by Him, and without Him was not anything made that was made" (John 1:1–3).

We as believers come to a group of men who look forward into the future. H. G. Wells writes of things to come, and how fearfully and wonderfully they are made. The best of the world's thinkers see chaos ahead; war and the passing of civilization. We ask: "What do you see in the future?" "We see confusion, we see the end of an era." Well, we see the Lord Jesus Christ through our telescope, and we see the kingdoms of this world become the kingdoms of our Lord and of His Christ, and righteousness covering the earth as the waters cover the sea, at the return of our Lord.

Then we go to the scientists and philosophers and say: "What do you see from your little mountain top?" Sir James Jeans says: "We see that behind the universe there is—something." And Mr. Eddington ponders and says: "Yes, definitely, and it is a mathematical something." How wonderful! But looking through the Word of God we find a Father pitying His children, sending His Son Christ to redeem and save the world from sin.

The psychologists take us to their little summit and bid us look within our own being. We say: "What have you found?" A psychologist in one of our universities wrote a book called "The Beast Within," and he tells young people that they have atavisms from their ancestors, who went in the forests on all fours,

and that if they do not want to have too many difficulties, they must not inhibit those ancestral strains,
that when the beast rages in his cage, it is best to take
him out for a walk, but discreetly. Thus our young
people are taught to go the way of the godless.

But we go to the Word of God and we find all our
comeliness in the dust before Him. We see, not a
beast from the forest, but rebellious creatures who
have disobeyed God, and who are not willing to
accept that which He offers in Christ, and we learn
to see that in man, that is, in the flesh, dwelleth no
good thing. Thus we are prepared to take the righteousness that is offered to us in Christ. The Scriptures
reveal to us the past and the future in a clarity that is
divine. They show us God, they show us ourselves.
All this gives great stability to the Christian life. This
makes it possible for us to walk uprightly, standing in
Jesus Christ in absolute certainty, with our minds at
peace in Him in the midst of life.

There is a fifth point which we can mention only
in passing. A knowledge of the Scriptures keeps us
from the counterfeits that are so prevalent in our day.
I am reminded of a story that appeared recently in
one of our weeklies. A young man took a young lady
to the theater, and afterwards they went to a night
club. They danced for hours in that atmosphere of
smoke and stale beer, and it was in the freshness of
the dawn that they left the place. "What is that smell?"
asked the young lady, as they came out. "That's not
a smell," replied the young man. "That is fresh air!"
There are some people today who have spent so much
time in the musty atmosphere of form, ceremony,

ritual, and religion, that when the Gospel is preached, they say: "What new thing is that?" It is not new, it is simply Christianity. The man who has lived his life in the country knows fresh air, and the man who is really taught in the Word of God will easily detect any counterfeit. It is a great thing to have the stability of the Word of God.

These words are for the young Christians who are just beginning the Christian life, and are the prospectus of an elementary course in sanctification which will lead on to the deeper truths that we must learn when we go in for our Master's degree in sanctification. But though we have not touched upon these deeper truths, they do exist.

God tells us in Hebrews 5 why some people find it rather difficult to take in the deeper truths of sanctification. The writer of the letter to the Hebrews wanted to tell them about Melchizedek. He seems to approach that truth, and then turn away from it, and then go toward it again, as much as to say: "I have something to tell you that I find most difficult." He talks about Melchizedek in verse 6, again in verse 10. It seems, then, as though the teaching problem were too great for him. He says: "Of him we have many things to say and hard to be uttered"—because the audience is stupid —(that is my own translation)—"and hard to be uttered, seeing that ye are dull of hearing."

We are all in that audience. These truths of the eternal High Priesthood of Christ are most important, but God the Holy Spirit says His ministers have difficulty in preaching them. Why? Because we are so dull of hearing, and fail, therefore, in receiving them.

If we wish the deeper truths, learn from the last verse in this chapter: "But strong meat belongeth to them that are of full age, even those who by reason of use have their senses exercised to discern both good and evil" (Heb. 5:14). It is by living in the Word of God, by studying from day to day, by learning, as David teaches us in the first Psalm, to delight ourselves in the Word of God, and in His law to meditate day and night, that we shall have our senses exercised to discernment. The phrase "to meditate day and night," is a Hebraism. It does not mean you are to be in cloistered seclusion reading morning, noon, and night, and never going out into the world. It means that in the midst of the most ceaseless activity in university, in home, in business, wherever we may be in the plan of God, that we are to live our lives within the sphere and boundaries of this Book. That gives us all the space we need to move around comfortably, for it takes us from eternity to eternity, and from the depths of our sin to the heights of God. He says: "Live there in the bounds of the Book and you shall grow in Christ."

May we not join Christ in His High Priestly prayer: "Make them holy through Thy truth: Thy Word is truth." And then we shall exclaim: "Make me thus holy, O Lord!"

Chapter 2

KNOWING THE POWER
OF HIS LOVE

"For the love of Christ constraineth us; because we thus judge, that if One died for all, then were all dead. And that He died for all that they which live should not henceforth live unto themselves, but unto Him which died for them, and rose again" (2 Cor. 5:14, 15).

ONE of the principles that run through the New Testament is that God expects the Christian to live a Christian life. Spiritual Christians know this, but some find it strange, because so many try to make detours around some of the plain commands that are in the Scripture. All through the Word of God the principle is laid down that after we have been saved in the Lord Jesus Christ, God wants the life of Christ to be lived and worked out practically in our day-by-day experience. Peter tells us: "Even hereunto were ye called: because Christ also suffered for us, leaving us an example, that ye should follow His steps" (1 Pet. 2:21). Now we know very well that the unsaved man cannot profit by an example; he is lost, and all the

examples in the world can never save him. When a
man is born again, however, God plants within him
the power or the genius to live the life of Christ.

There have been some artists who dissipated their
gifts and did not create for the world all that was within
the limits of their capacity. Likewise there are Christians who dissipate the gift of the Christ-life and do not
live up to the capacity which God has given them.
That does not alter the fact that God has given to each
one of us, who are believers, that divine genius of life in
Christ, and that one of the fundamental principles of
the New Testament is that He expects Christians to live
Christ.

Consider the call of God to holy living found in our
text, a text addressed to a limited group. When one is
staying with other people in the same house, and the
postman brings the mail in the morning, one does not
take up promiscuously any envelope one sees, slit it
open and begin to read it. One looks very carefully to
see that one's name is on the envelope before opening
it; it is considered extremely bad manners to open anyone else's letters. Now, in the Word of God there are
texts addressed to everybody in the world, and there are
texts that are specifically addressed to certain people.
Do not think that everything in the Bible is for everybody in the world, for that is not true. There are many
things said only to those who have been born again.
If an unsaved man tries to live by Christian promises
he will make a complete failure of his efforts. Frequently in our churches, when the minister gives his
message with a desire to help the people of God, unsaved people come in; they listen to a declaration of

courage, faith, and hope, and they say to themselves:
"I should like to have a little more courage, a little
more faith, and a little more hope," but they have not
been born again, and it is as impossible in spiritual
things for them to walk before they have been born as
it is in the earthly sphere.

Our text is limited in its address: "For the love of
Christ constraineth us." Who are the "us"? It is addressed to those who were once dead but who are now
alive. "We thus judge: that if One died for all, then
were all dead: and that He died for all, that they
which live should not henceforth live unto themselves."
Ask yourself this question: Am I alive in Christ? If so,
this message is directed to you. If not, you cannot live
unto Him. "The carnal mind is enmity against God;
it is not subject to the law of God, nor indeed can it be.
So then they that are in the flesh cannot please God"
(Rom. 8:7, 8). "The natural man receiveth not the
things of the Spirit of God, for they are foolishness unto
him: neither can he know them, because they are
spiritually discerned" (1 Cor. 2:14). All these things
and more are said of those who are dead in trespasses
and sins. If we are to be constrained by the love of
Christ, we must realize that, in addressing us thus, He
addresses us as those who were once dead, but who are
now alive.

Some time ago, out in China, I heard the story of a
Chinese evangelist who spoke of the weight of sin. A
heckler in the crowd said: "How much is this weight
of sin? Is it 50 pounds or 100 pounds?" Quick as a
flash the Chinese preacher answered: "If you put a
weight upon the chest of a corpse, whether it was 50

pounds or 100 pounds, he would not know the difference." So the unsaved man does not know the weight
of sin. Now and again, he may feel a little remorse, but
there is a great deal of difference between remorse and
repentance. Remorse weeps for lost innocence, regret-
ting that it no longer has the innocence with which to
go out into sin afresh, but repentance weeps in the presence of God, because it has grieved the One who is
righteous and who is holy. God tells us that we were
dead, and that He brought us out into life. "And you
hath He quickened, who were dead in trespasses and
sins; wherein in time past ye walked according to the
course of this world, according to the prince of the
power of the air, the spirit that now worketh in the
children of disobedience" (Eph. 2:1, 2). With this in
mind we must realize that our text is addressed to those
who know that once they were dead—that is easy to
know—and who know just as surely that now they are
alive. Do you know that you are alive in Christ? That
is the only knowledge that will permit true growth in
the Christian life.

Secondly, this text teaches us, the resurrected people
in Christ, that those who live in Christ have a new
faculty which they did not before possess—the faculty
of spiritual judgment. "We thus judge." This faculty
of judgment in the Christian life is one of great im-
portance. It comes because the life that is ours is the
life of Christ. We read (in 1 Cor. 1:30): "But of Him
are ye in Christ Jesus, who of God is made unto us wis-
dom." Thus we are able to comprehend even in our
own lives, that which before we were not able to
comprehend. Then in the 2nd chapter of the same

epistle we read: "But he that is spiritual judgeth or discerneth all things, yet he himself is judged of no man. For who hath known the mind of the Lord, that He may instruct him? But we have the mind of Christ (v. 15, 16). That is the reason we are able to judge sin; that is the reason we are able to judge ourselves, and know how we should live.

Now, since we are going to speak about judging ourselves, I want to take just a moment to point out the fact that we are not to judge others. It is so easy to talk about the sins of other people and to judge them. I know some people whose capacity for the judgment of others is very highly developed, and some of us might wish that it could be developed concerning themselves! I know a woman in Philadelphia who is sometimes severe with the young people of this generation. She does not understand them at all. One evening I went into the church for a special prayer group, where about a dozen people met. When I opened the door she said: "Ah, here he comes; we will ask him," and she said: "Do you think it is right for Christian young women to put powder on their faces?" Well, I had an Irish great-grandmother, and sometimes the Irish strain comes out in me, and I answered quickly, without reflecting at all, and without attempting to decide the matter: "Well, if in David's day it was the fashion to put oil on the face to make it shine, and if it is the fashion today to put on powder to take the shine off, I do not see that it makes any great difference!" All these things really depend on the lordship of Christ in the individual life. Christians can always honor the Lord by looking their best, but each individual will know without question whether what is seen in the mirror is dominated by the Lord or ruled by self. Let our judgment be for ourselves, and not for others, thus we will become more like the Lord Jesus Christ.

Sin, as you know, is not merely the commission of iniquity, it is anything that is contrary to the will of God, and therefore sin in one life may be quite different from sin in another. Of course, I am not speaking of iniquity, of things which are not even named among the gentiles. The Word of God gives us clear definition of things which are sin in any life. Did you ever stop to think that going to too many meetings might be a sin in some cases? I had a young lady in one of my meetings at home, whose mother came to me and said: "I wish you would say a word to my daughter. We have had a very bad report from her school about her work. She has become interested in Christian Endeavor, and on Monday evening she goes to a committee meeting, on Tuesday evening she goes to a rally of some kind, on Wednesday evening she attends a social group, and on Thursday evening she goes to something else. Her algebra has gone down so much that the teacher says she may have to drop the class." I turned to the young lady and said: "There is a danger of your becoming religiously intoxicated; you will have to stop going to meetings so much, and get on with the work which is your present duty. You must get through your classes in a way that will honor and glorify the Lord and give you the witness of good scholarship before your teachers." Perhaps you never thought that going to a meeting might be a sin, but in this young lady's case going to a meeting was sin, for she was

doing too much of it, in the wrong way. Perhaps there
are some people who are sinning in just the opposite
way. The Word of God says in the epistle to the Hebrews: "Forsake not the assembling of yourselves together, as the manner of some is" (Heb. 10:25). So
we must be ready to judge ourselves severely, and be
willing to move in whatever way our Lord directs.

Thirdly, we find that there is constraint here—
"The love of Christ constraineth us." We are driven
on. It is that constraining force which activates this
faculty of judgment which God has given to us. The
Christian has become a son of God, and in that
capacity has been raised to the nobility of Heaven.
Just as the aristocracy of the centuries has created the
motto, "*Noblesse oblige*," so it is that the very fact of
bearing the Name of Christ should force us toward
Him. A being who is a child of God should live as a
child of God. If we are to be of Heaven's royalty, we
should learn to live regally; a king should live like a
king.

Some time ago our newspapers in America contained references to a monarch on the Continent who
was living in a way that caused even the world to
ridicule his fashion of life; he scandalized the world by
his actions. Someone said: "What could you expect?
His great-grandfather was a swineherd who took the
throne." But the real reason at the back of it all was
not the fact that the man's great-grandfather was a
swineherd; it was the fact that he, like every one else,
had an old nature. Whether you give to your old
nature the courage of the playing field of some great
public school, or the tonal accent of some university,

does not matter; it is not a question of the polish of the old nature; it is a question of letting the new nature exercise its royal sovereignty. The old nature cannot be bred out by any Mendelian selection. We cannot, by giving people proper ancestors, bring them to Christ. It is a question not of race, but of grace. It is the supernatural life, and, when once we have been born again, our nobility must be a factor in our lives, constraining us to live in keeping with that which we are in Christ.

Next, we come to the very heart and the most important part of this text. We are led to the judgment scene. "We thus judge." One of the most impressive sights in the world is a High Court of Justice. You see the judge with his wig and his magnificent robes taking his seat in solemn pomp to pass upon the highest affairs of the tribunal, and it is indeed a scene that causes the respect of every right thinking person who desires justice and judgment. Here we have before us such a scene. "We thus judge." We are to sit upon the bench. Whom are we to judge? We are to judge ourselves. That causes us to realize that there are within ourselves two natures: we have an old nature and we have a new nature. It is this very gift of Christ that enters into all believers. Our text teaches us that the enmity between these two natures must be settled in court. The prisoner must be brought to the bar. The new life that is Christ within us must bring to the bar of judgment of Christ all that is within us of the old nature, that it may be delivered over for crucifixion. As we search the Word of God, we find the terms of the indictment that we shall bring against ourselves in this judgment scene. We find that we are sinners by choice, and that we are sinners by divine decree.

Some people do not like the teaching of the Word of God that we are sinners by nature. A man says to me: "Oh, do you believe in total depravity?" "Yes, I do," I reply. Then he says: "That there is no good at all in man?" That is not the same thing at all. I believe in total depravity, but there is a great deal of good in man. The point is merely this, that the good which is in man cannot be accepted in Heaven. A man may be a millionaire in character and that will buy him a high position in this country and in this world, but when he crosses the frontier to go to Heaven it is a debased coinage and God cannot accept it at all. That is the reason why we believe in total depravity. It is not that there is no good in the human heart outside of Christ; there is a devotion and there is an honor among unsaved people that frequently Christians would do well to emulate in their own lives. But there is no doubt that the new nature, which is the life of Christ, is an entirely different thing. It is Christ Himself. God says that we were conceived in sin and shapen in iniquity. Some people do not like to believe that. I remember a woman came to me once and said: "Do you believe my little baby, who is one year old, is a sinner?" I said to her: "I want to tell you a story about my own little child. I have a little girl who, when she was only about nine months old, told a lie before she could talk." So I told her how it happened. My little girl was born in France, where we were living while I was studying at a university there. We had a French maid, who taught her a nursery rhyme, which was this:

Ainsi font, font, font,
Les petites marionettes;
Ainsi font, font, font,
Trois petits tours
Et puis s'en vont.

She moved her baby fingers at the words of that little
French nursery rhyme. It was a cute little trick, and
you know how parents are with their small children,
they have great joy in their baby ways. Many a time
we had laughed with her and kissed her when she did
this. But she also sucked her thumb, and many a time
I had taken her little hand and slapped it gently when
I found her doing this. One day I came into the room
and she had a wet thumb and was just moving it towards her mouth. She saw me, and she immediately
began to wave her hands about. It was just as though
she had said: "Daddy, you are quite mistaken. I
wasn't going to suck my thumb at all. I was acting that
nice little marionette rhyme which delights you so
much!" The worst of it was that the Bible told me she
had inherited that nature from her father! Eve may be
blamed in the comic papers but in the Bible it says
"as in Adam all die," and "by one man sin entered."
The responsibility was plainly there, and I knew that
she and I, and all our fathers and mothers before us,
were sinners by nature. Sin is within, and we must
realize that the new man in Christ Jesus must sit in
judgment upon the old nature that is within. We must
realize that the roots of all sin, of all iniquity, are
within us, and that the only way to deal with that old
nature is to condemn it in such judgment, the love of
Christ constraining us to the judgment.

If Christ had to go to the cross and die it was because we were dead—sinners by nature, but this is not all. Because we are sinners by nature we became sinners by choice. We did not stop all our evil doing when we reached the age of one. It was not merely that the root was within us in childhood. As we grew and developed in life all of us came to the stage when very definitely we chose that which was sin. We are told in the first epistle of John, chapter 1, that if we say "we have no sin" we deceive ourselves; but that if we say: "Oh, yes, I have an old nature, but I have brought it to the stage where it does not work any more," God says we make Him a liar and His Word is not in us.

There is only one thing we can do, and that is to accept God's verdict that we are sinners by nature, and that we are sinners by choice, and that God has declared us, therefore, under the divine decree of His wrath. We sin solely because we are sinners. We must live in the courtroom. That is the solution, for it will bring us to the very heart of victory in Christ Jesus. We must take up our position with the Judge on the bench and agree to His verdict. "We thus judge," and moment by moment and day by day we consent that our old nature and all that is associated with it should be brought into judgment before the Lord Jesus Christ. We deliver it over to be crucified and, as Paul says, we die daily. Paul had to condemn himself, daily deliver himself over to crucifixion, once more tell the Judge who sat with him on the bench that his old nature must be kept in constant death in the place of execution, so that he might live thus in the death of Christ. And so must we.

ien we must give consideration to the love that
rains. "The love of Christ constraineth us." How
are we to speak of the love of Christ? I must confess
that here I am in a dilemma. We must go on with the
text and talk about the love of Christ, but the Word of
God tells us very definitely that the love of Christ
passeth knowledge. In the epistle to the Ephesians Paul
says: "That ye may be able to comprehend what is the
breadth, and length, and depth, and height, and to
know the love of Christ, which passeth knowledge."
It is something like a boy in school, who on going to
the blackboard to work out a problem in mathematics,
hears his teacher say: "Now we are working on the
question of the ratio of the circumference to the radius
of a circle, and I want you to find exactly what that
is." Mathematicians call it π, and they have worked it
out at 3.141–, and then, for want of anything better,
they have put 3.1416, instead of 3.14159285—and so
on. I saw recently in a paper a table published by the
Royal Society in London in which a mathematician
in England had worked out π to the two-thousandth
place; it was just a great block of figures right across
the paper, yet still there were more to follow. Mathematicians know that you cannot square a circle; you
go on and on and on, and the problem never ends.
Paul says to the Ephesians: "I want you to know that
love of Christ which passeth knowledge—I want you
to know something that cannot be known." That is the
problem that God puts up to us very definitely—to
know something that cannot be known. Yet in the
measure that we comprehend the love of Christ; in
the measure that we fix our gaze upon the cross; in the

measure that we see what it meant for Him who was
rich to become poor for our sakes, that we through His
poverty might be made rich; in the measure that we
enter into this great love of Christ; in that measure we
are going to be constrained. As we grow in knowledge
of that love, we shall judge more truly, we shall act
more definitely with our old nature, we shall be more
unsparing with the flesh. We shall enter more into the
life of Christ as the love of Christ constrains us. And as
we grow in knowledge of this love that passeth knowledge, so shall we be filled unto all the fulness of God.

In the King James' Version, the words are: "That
ye might be filled with all the fulness of God" (Eph.
3:19). In the Mississippi valley there are many millions
of people who have never seen the ocean. Every once
in a while people make the trip East and come to one
of our shore resorts to get a glimpse of the ocean. Their
friends at home always say to them: "Take a good
look at the ocean, so that you can describe it when you
get back." Now suppose a man went down to the
shore of Atlantic City with a pint bottle, and dipped
the bottle in the ocean and filled it with the fulness of
the ocean. Suppose he took that bottle back to Kansas
and said: "You asked me to describe the ocean, but
instead of that I have brought it back to you." How
foolish he would be. Anyone who knew the sea would
say: "That is not the ocean; that is a pint of stale salt
water." How could you have in the bottle the thousands of waves that beat upon the strand, that dash
themselves against the rocks? How could you see the
warm tropical sea of indescribable blue, with the
white waves foaming up the beach as the palm trees

bend above them? How could you see those placid
days in mid-ocean as the prow of the ship cuts its way
through the waters? How could you put all that in a
bottle? Paul's problem must have been similar when
he wrote to the Ephesians: "I am praying that you
might know the love of Christ that cannot be known,
that you might be filled unto all the fulness of Christ"
—"unto," not "with." You can fill your bottle with
one little dip into the ocean, but to put all of the ocean
into the bottle is quite a different thing; a miracle
would be required there. Now, says God, that is the
miracle of the Christian life. That which is unknow-
able, that which is the mathematical formula that
never ends, you can find in your life; it will grow
within you, and as it grows and grows, you begin to
realize more of the riches of all that is there in the
mathematical formula, in the wonder of the unknown,
in the sea and all that is therein. Then you realize that
this love of Christ which cannot be fully known is becoming known. Little by little we learn it; thus more
and more it constrains us.

Last of all, we must see that this love of Christ constrains us in a very definite direction. We have been
living to ourselves. We are taken off that road and
put on the road that leads to Him. Living unto ourselves describes the life of the carnal Christian. After
describing the unsaved man as being "the natural
man" who "receiveth not the things of the Spirit,"
the apostle describes the Christian who has been living
unto himself as being filled with envy, strife, and di-
vision. He then adds: "Are ye not carnal, and walk
as men?" (1 Cor. 3:3). That is to say: "Are ye not

carnal and walk as the unsaved man?" It is hard to
tell the difference between your life and that of the
man who has not been born again. It is from this
road that the love of Christ constrains us. Because of
His death for us, because of that amazing revelation of
His love, we are drawn into the new path of living
unto Him. We become spiritual Christians, to use the
language of the apostle once more. We have judged
our carnal mind and delivered it over to death; the
mind of Christ, which we have, is thus allowed full
play. Christ liveth in us; thus we live unto Him. May
God grant us today so to see the love of Christ that we
may be constrained to this judgment, and that we
shall walk with our lives directed unto Him.

Chapter 3

PURIFYING YOURSELF
IN THE BLESSED HOPE

*Every man that hath this hope in Him, purifieth himself,
even as He is pure"* (1 John 3:3).

THE world has a proverb, "While there's life
there's hope." The Bible teaches that where there
is hope there is life. We read in 1 John 3:2, 3: "Beloved, now are we the sons of God; and it doth not yet
appear what we shall be: but we know that, when He
shall appear, we shall be like Him; for we shall see
Him as He is. And every man that hath this hope in
Him purifieth himself, even as He is pure." This
purifying power of the blessed hope is that which will
occupy our attention.

The early Church lived in the light of the thought
of the Lord's return. At night they closed their eyes in
sleep, thinking: Perhaps before morning our Lord
will be at the door and call us to be with Himself. In
the morning when they awakened it was with the
thought: "Today, perhaps, the Lord Jesus will call us

to be with Himself." They laid down their lives in martyrdom, and undoubtedly many of them thought, as they went toward the block or toward the arena and the lions: "Would not it be wonderful, if, before the ax could fall, or before the animals were released, the Lord Jesus should call us to be with Himself, and the unbelieving crowd should see that we are no longer there." That gave life and power to the Church. They were always thinking: At any moment our Lord may be here, and the miracle of the first phase of His return shall come to pass. "The dead in Christ shall rise first, then we which are alive and remain shall be caught up together with them in the clouds to meet the Lord in the air, and so shall we ever be with the Lord" (1 Thes. 4:16, 17). This hope was in no small measure responsible for the first love of that Church, whose members were so willing to die for the Lord.

The points of our message are very simple. First, He shall appear; secondly, we shall be like Him; thirdly, we shall see Him; and the conclusion is that every one who believes these things is going to live differently, because these truths are possessing the heart.

First of all, let us look at the words "He shall appear." Oh, how many men have written foolish things about the coming of the Lord! We must insist that we have nothing whatsoever in common with anyone who tries in any wise to set any date for the coming of the Lord. We know not the day, nor the hour, nor the time, nor the season. I once happened to pick up a book, and read in it the prophecy, which the writer said the Lord had revealed to him, that Christ would appear the following year. In the next edition, after the time

had passed, the writer merely added a preface, and
said: "I was mistaken, but the Lord had graciously
permitted me to see that I made a mistake in my
calculations; but He has now permitted me to say most
positively that it will be next year." The Bible says
that if a man prophesies and it does not come to pass,
we shall know that he is prophesying lies. Do not believe any man who in any wise commits himself to any
system of dates in prophetic interpretation. "In such
an hour as ye think not, the Son of Man cometh"
(Lk. 12:40).

Some have said that the second coming of Christ is
the conversion of the sinner, that it was the Day of
Pentecost, that it was the destruction of Jerusalem, and
many other like things, but it is none of these. When
He comes many things shall take place that have not
yet been and that are not now. The dead in Christ
shall rise, and the living shall be changed and be made
like unto the Lord. His kingdom shall be brought
from Heaven and be established on earth. How we re-
joice to know that He shall appear and shall set right
all that is so terribly wrong upon the earth! The
Church in the Middle Ages was like the dog in Æsop's
Fables, which, passing over a bridge with a bone in its
mouth, saw its reflection, and opening its mouth to
seize the bone in the reflection, lost the bone that it had.
The church in the Middle Ages, looking at power
round about it, and desiring to have a kingdom, gave
up the blessed hope and the true heavenly calling, and
began to seek temporal power. That horrible thing,
ecclesiastical ambition, came into its own, and the
church has been the poorer ever since because of it.

But when we get away from that and realize that we
are a heavenly people with a heavenly hope, looking
for the coming of our Lord Jesus who shall appear,
then all our work will be better, for we shall be in line
with that which the Lord Himself has called us to do.
In this present age He is taking out a people for His
Name. Some are always trying to build a kingdom
that shall be a mere earthly kingdom, but that is
not what God is doing today. He is calling out the
Church, not building a kingdom. There will be no
kingdom till He comes.

A few years ago I was out in the western plains of
America, in the State of Montana. In those flat prairies
one can see a great distance, and the road lay straight
ahead of us for miles without a bend. Far away I saw a
speck, and as we came nearer I saw it was a man who
was bending over, pumping air into a tire. He did not
seem to be making much headway. When I got up to
him I stopped and said: "Perhaps you would like to
use my pump." He replied: "My pump is all right,
but I am afraid there is a hole in my tire!" There he
was, pumping air into a tire which had a hole in it!

You know, dear friends, there is so much Christian
work that is just like that. You see men slaving away,
and you ask them: "What are you doing?" and they
reply: "Oh, we are bringing in the kingdom!" They
are trying to bring in the kingdom, but they are
doomed to failure. Only the King will do that. You
are not going to Christianize Moscow, or Tokyo, or
Chicago, or London. You are not going to Christianize
Foreign Offices and the Stock Exchanges. If you read
the Sermon on the Mount to those people it would

have exactly the same effect as if you took the eleventh chapter of Isaiah to the Zoological Gardens and insisted that the lion should lie down with the lamb, and that the lion should eat straw like the ox. Yes, that will come to pass some day, but not until He has come and set all things right. He shall appear, and then all shall be put in order. Then shall come the righteousness and the peace which He has promised to the earth.

The coming of the Lord is a series of events, and its climax is the establishment of His kingdom. Until He comes we need not expect to see it. The first coming of the Lord was a series of events, thirty-three years long, and likewise the second coming of the Lord is also a series of events. The first coming of the Lord was the annunciation by an angel to a virgin, it was the bringing forth of the Lord in a manger at Bethlehem, it was the anointing of Christ by the Spirit for His work and ministry as He went about doing good. The first coming of Christ was the death of a Man upon the cross; it was an open grave and an ascent in the clouds; it was thirty-three years long. A great many people, however, are very confused about prophecy because they think of the second coming of Christ merely as one flashing moment. There shall be a flashing moment just as "the lightning cometh out of the east and shineth even unto the west," but the coming of the Lord is much more than that.

It is related that in a Bible School one of the students was being examined on the subject of prophecy, and the examiner said to the young man: "Before the Lord sets up His reign on the earth, what must take place?" The young man replied: "The reign of the Antichrist and the great tribulation." "Yes," said the examiner, "that is correct. And what must take place before the great tribulation?" "The taking out of all the believers," said the young man. "Yes, that is correct. And what must happen before the taking out of the believers?" The young man said: "Nothing but the shout." That is the truth of God, dear friends—nothing but the shout. "The Lord Himself shall descend from Heaven with a shout, with the voice of the archangel and the trump of God" (1 Thes. 4:16), and then this great series of events will be inaugurated, all of which are bound up in the related truths of the coming of the Lord. His return is the answer to the world's problems.

One day friends took me from London down through Essex, and, reaching the little town of Epping, we turned round a bend in the road, and saw before us a billboard with bills prominently displayed. My eye caught this sentence: "If the U.N. fails, what?" and next to it there was another bill: "Behold, I come quickly!" I could not help thinking that, perhaps by accident, or perhaps by the deliberate action of the man who stuck up the bills, and who knew Christian truth, those two bills had been very properly placed. This world has only question marks when it comes to the problems that confront us. The answer is with God, and He is upon the throne, and in His own good moment He will bring to pass that which He has ordained.

Secondly, we consider the phrase: "We shall be like Him." To my mind, that phrase is perhaps the most breath-taking in all literature. It is to be compared only with the phrase that may be greater because it makes all else possible: "He loved us." In those two phrases, "He loved us," and "we shall be like Him," we have two of the greatest wonders of the universe, and undoubtedly those two thoughts shall occupy our hearts long after eternity has begun for us. He loved us, and He shall make us like Himself. What does it mean, that we shall be like Him?

First, we shall be like Him in His holiness. If I could have only one attribute of Jesus Christ—thank God we will not be thus limited—I am sure that I would rather be like Him in His holiness than in anything else. We shall be like Him in holiness. How we need it! We have a wonderful story from the life of Peter given us in the 13th chapter of John's Gospel. You remember that when the Lord started to wash the disciples' feet, Peter drew back and said: "Lord, Thou shalt never wash my feet!" and the Lord said: "If I wash thee not, thou hast no part with Me." Then Peter said: "Lord, not my feet only, but also my hands and my head." Jesus answered: "He that is washed needeth not save to wash his feet, but is clean every whit." The Lord was stating the principle that when a man is born again and saved, he cannot be born again, and again, and again; once forever he has been justified, has been looked upon in the righteousness of Christ. God sees him in all the perfection of His Son.

He that is washed needs not to be washed again. The Lord Jesus was saying to Peter: "I see thee in My own righteousness." But there must be the daily cleansing. Peter learned that and knew it well, and we must learn the same. Day by day we must go back to the presence of the Lord to be cleansed. "If we confess

our sins, He is faithful and just to forgive us our sins,
and to cleanse us from all unrighteousness" (1 John
1:9). The day is to come, however, when we shall no
longer have to bow down in the evening and say:
"Lord, the old nature has broken out again. Lord,
Thou seest my daily and hourly need to be crucified
with Thee." We shall be like Him. Is it any wonder
that in the book of Revelation the elders cast down
their golden crowns when they see the glassy sea and
realize that there will never be need of confession of
sin again? You remember the verse of the hymn:

> Holy, holy, holy, all the saints adore Thee,
> Casting down their golden crowns around the glassy sea.

Why did they cast their crowns at that particular
place? Well, when Solomon built his Temple he made
a laver that was called a sea. It was the symbol of
cleansing. It stood between the altar, where the blood
was shed, and the tabernacle, where the worship of
God was centered. The priests who had been cleansed
from their sin by the shedding of the blood came to be
cleansed from their sins in that water in the laver. It
was a symbol, just as the washing of Peter's feet
was a symbol, that you and I as Christians must day by
day and moment by moment creep back to the cross.
We must ever remember that when we have done our
very best, when, yielded to Christ, we have been able
to pass a whole day without conscious sin, that even
then, at the best we are unprofitable servants and still
must confess that in ourselves there dwelleth no good
thing. But God tells us that in the heavenly temple the
sea shall be turned to crystal; no longer will there need

to be water to cleanse us; there shall be no more sea; there will be no more sins to be confessed.

I am quite sure that when we come to that heavenly temple we shall be reminded by the sea that has been turned to crystal that we shall never have any more sin to confess, that it has been taken away for ever, every root gone. The Lord Jesus when He spoke of Satan, said: "The prince of this world cometh and findeth nothing in Me." You and I must say: "The prince of this world cometh and findeth plenty in me." There is in our hearts an ally of Satan, like the wooden horse of Troy, all ready to let the enemy come in if we are not on the watch. But the day will come when that old nature shall be removed, and we shall be able to say that there is nothing left of sin within us. Thus sin can never break out in the universe again. How glad we shall be to cast down any crowns we may have around that reminder of the end of sin, and from holy hearts like His, cry:

> Lord, Thy glory fills the Heaven;
>   Earth is with its fulness stored;
> Unto Thee be glory given,
>   Holy, holy, holy, Lord.

Then, too, we are going to be like Him in His love. How cold we are, how unloving! He really loves souls. Can we say we do? I wonder if you have seen that little leaflet, several millions of which have been printed, called "Suppose!" The writer asks: "Suppose someone offered you 1000 dollars for every soul that you tried to lead to Christ, would you be more diligent than you are today? If you would be more diligent in soul-winning if someone gave you 1000 dollars for

every soul that you tried to lead to Christ, can it be
that you love dollars more than you love souls?" How
quickly such a thing reveals the hearts of men! But
our Lord Jesus Christ loved us. How He loved; and
we shall be like Him in that love. Self shall be put
away, and His love will be ours.

We shall also be like Him in His power. In the 2nd
Psalm we have that great passage that speaks of His
returning. Our Lord says that He shall break the
nations with a rod of iron and dash them to pieces as a
potter's vessel. Yet, in the 2nd chapter of Revelation it
says of believers: "And he that overcometh, to him
will I give power over the nations. And he shall rule
them with a rod of iron; as the vessels of a potter shall
they be broken in pieces" (5:26, 27). The prospect is
given to us to be associated with the Messiah in His
reign, to sit upon His throne, and to be the instruments
of His rule. How wonderful that we shall be like Him
in His power!

In the third place, not only shall He appear, and
not only shall we be like Him, but we shall see Him as
He is. It would seem that this sight of the Lord is the
cause of our being made like Him, as though the vision
of Him in all His eternal glory, no longer hidden with
the veil of the flesh but eternally transfigured, would
have in it that which shall transform us, making us
like unto Himself. In that day when we see Him how
much there will be to say!

> Then we shall be where we would be;
> Then we shall be what we should be;
> Things which are not now, nor could be,
>   Then shall be our own.

And we shall be able to say what we should like to say
to Him then. When two people fall in love with each
other, and both know it, then they like to talk about it.
Who saw the other first? "When Mrs. So-and-So
brought me across the room to present me to you,
what did you think? I liked you from the beginning!
What did you think about me?" They also argue with
each other as to who fell in love with the other first.
When we see our Lord there will be many things to
hear and say, but while we shall love to talk about how
He came and how He loved us, there will never be any
argument as to who was loved first. We read that He
loved the ungodly, and that we love Him because He
first loved us.

> He saw me ruined in the fall,
> And loved me notwithstanding all;
> He saved me from my lost estate;
> His loving-kindness, O, how great!

Oh! the joy of seeing Him! Ten thousand times greater
than any earthly joy will be that sight of our Lord and
Master, Jesus Christ.

Some criticize those who talk about seeing the Lord.
I have heard people assail the hymn, "O that will be
glory for me!" There is a sense, of course, in which
such thoughts may be mere sentimental emotion. But
there is a present power in such a hope. The Bible tells
us in this text of ours: "Every man that hath this hope
purifieth himself." Let me set before you two attitudes,
both of which are held by some believers in these days
of our Lord's absence. In 1917, when the United
States entered into the Great War, there was a young

couple in the West who had made their plans to be
married. They had a little house which they had been
furnishing for weeks, and all their resources had gone
into the preparation of that home. Their plan had been
to be married and to move into this new little home,
but war was declared, and the young man, who
was a reserve officer, was immediately called to the
troops. His company was ordered to go to the Mexican
frontier to train before going to France. The young
lady said to him the day before he was due to go on:
"It is not quite the date for our wedding, but you
might be ordered overseas immediately; you might be
killed, and thus I might never see you again. I would a
thousand times rather go through life bearing your
name than go through life always explaining that the
man I loved had been killed in the war. So let us go
through with it and be married right now." So they
were quietly married, and for their honeymoon he
went with the troops and she went to the little house.
She was very lonely, of course, and you can well
imagine how she missed her lover-husband! Day after
day he wrote to her, and the letters began to accumu-
late. He sent her gifts; a Navajo rug, some Mexican
lace, and some Indian pottery. Months passed, and
there came an afternoon when she felt especially
lonely. She took some pillows and put them on the
floor in front of the open fireplace, spread the rug upon
the floor and sat down upon it. She took the box with
all her husband's letters; on some pillows she spread
the lace that he had sent her, and put the pottery on a
chair before her. Then, taking two or three hand-
kerchiefs for a good cry, she settled down to enjoy her-

self with his letters and with thoughts of him. But, as she began reading the letters and thinking of him, suddenly there was a step on the porch, the door opened, and he was there. He had sent a telegram and it had been delayed in delivery, as so frequently happened in those war days. When she saw him and the realization came to her that he was there, she jumped to her feet; the letters in her lap were scattered all over the place, some of them falling into the fire; she stepped on the lace, and knocked a piece of pottery off the chair, but she was in his arms, and that mattered more to her than all the letters and all the gifts he ever could have sent her. He had returned. She had him, and having him, had all. Before I draw the analogy, which you have already seen, let me tell you another story.

When I first set foot on English soil, in the days when there were still food cards and when saccharine was being used, I wanted to get a newspaper, for I had been at sea, on a transport, for many days. I knew the name of only one newspaper in England, so I went to the newsstand and said: "I want a copy of the *Times*." Then I got into the railway carriage to go up to London, and as I looked at the paper I thought this was the most curious paper I had ever seen in the world. There were only advertisements on the front page, whereas in the States we have nothing but news on the front page. I turned over page after page, looking for the news, and finally, when I got to the fourth or fifth page, I saw some news, and I thought this must be the most important news in the world that day. But it was the report of a divorce case heard in London. I started to read it. It was the story of a young aristocrat who had married a girl and had then gone off to the trenches. She had written to him that she was occupied in war work, saying how tired she was with nursing in a certain hospital. She apologized for not writing frequently, saying that she was spending hours every day with the war wounded. Some months later her husband was coming on leave, and a friend of his, who had received information about the state of affairs, said to him: "I would not announce, if I were you, that I was getting leave; I would slip over quietly." The husband took his advice, arrived in London unannounced, and went to the hospital where the girl was supposed to be a nurse. He found she was not there at all! Then he found out where she was living, but on calling got no satisfaction, merely being told: "Oh, she will probably be at the tea dance at the Ritz this afternoon." He found her there, in the company of another man. He soon found out a great deal more, and the judge readily granted him a decree of divorce. I could not help contrasting those two stories and drawing the spiritual analogy.

Dear friends, our Lord Jesus is coming back and He is going to find you and He is going to find me in one of those two attitudes. Will you be flirting with the world, or will you be occupied with His love letters, His gifts, His work, thinking of Him? He is coming! "Every man that hath this hope in Him purifieth himself, even as He is pure." What a judgment that is going to be when He appears! Paul speaks of that moment, and we cannot wonder that he says: "Knowing the terror of the Lord, we persuade men." Those words were written to Christians; Paul was speaking of the judgment seat of Christ. Knowing what that white light of His holiness will be, when we see it, we persuade Christian men to be living in the light of His coming, to be remembering that our Lord is at the door, to be purifying themselves; for while in that judgment there may be no possibility of eternal condemnation for the redeemed who appear there, yet, nevertheless, there will be something so searching when we see our Lord, that Paul can speak of it as terror. John tells us to abide in Him, that we may "not be ashamed before Him at His Coming." How are we living? Shall we be ashamed? Blessed is the man whom when the Master cometh He shall find watching. Dr. Torrey used to say: "We must live as though He were coming this day, and plan and work as though He were not coming in our lifetime, for then as we work we shall not be ashamed before Him at His coming."

The last point is very brief. It is the conclusion of all the rest. He shall appear; we shall be like Him; we shall see Him. Belief in these things brings us strength to say: We shall seek to purify ourselves. "Every man that hath this hope purifieth himself."

How can we purify ourselves? We have such need of it. The answer is: We cannot do it ourselves. At the time of Shakespeare there was an English poet, Robert Herrick, who wrote a beautiful little quatrain, taking as the thought upon which he had made his lines that incident in Greek mythology of the labors of Hercules. Hercules was sent forth to do an impossible thing, to clean up the filthy stables of Augeas. Robert Herrick compares his heart to that stable, and writes:

> Lord, I confess that Thou alone art able
> To purify this Augean stable.
> Be the seas water and the lands all soap,
> Yet if Thy Blood not wash me, there's no hope.

What that old poet of England found is true, of course, for the unsaved man for salvation from sin, and it is true for the saved man for his sins. Man cannot purify himself. There must be that moment by moment yielding to the Lord. If you can have victory over sin for one minute, you can have victory over sin for two minutes. Continue yielding to the Lord, saying: "Lord, Jesus, this old nature must be crucified; Thy life must be my purity." If you can do this for two minutes, then you can do it for three minutes, and if you can do it for three minutes, you can go on for an hour, and then a day, and then a year. The old nature will still be there; it will still seek to break forth with at least one of the lusts of the flesh. The carnal mind is enmity against God, but our God has made provision for victory, and the sanctifying power of the Word, and the constraining force of His love are factors in it, and a belief in the return of our Lord Jesus Christ is one of the beliefs that will bring us closer to Himself. May we not say to ourselves: "Even so, come quickly, Lord Jesus, and I, who have this hope, must purify myself even as Thou art pure"?

Chapter 4

EXPERIENCING TRANSFORMATION
BY HIS SPIRIT

"But we all, with open face beholding as in a glass the glory of the Lord, are changed into the same image from glory to glory, even as by the Spirit of the Lord" (2 Cor. 3:18).

IN ONE of our Lord's parables we have the picture of a man who stands between God and men to get a blessing from the One and give it to the other. A friend came in the middle of the night, so the man had to get up and go out and knock on the door of a neighbor and ask for food for the guest who had come unexpectedly. I have been impressed by something which is to be found in that passage: the man who stood there to minister used the word "friend" twice as he knocked on the door. He said: "Friend! a friend has come to me in need, and I have nothing." If you and I as Christians are ever to be a blessing to any other person, it must be because we have that double friendship towards the world and its great need, and toward the Father. Our friendship with the world must not be, need we say it, that friendship which is enmity with our God; such friendship is treason. To warm our

64

hands at the world's fire is to betray Christ. But we must have that friendship with the world that loves souls for Christ's sake. And our friendship with God must be a close one. It is not to a casual acquaintance that we will go in the middle of the night to seek food for our guests. It is only to someone near that we will go with our cry: "Friend! . . . friend! . . . a friend has come . . . I have nothing!"

Someone comes in the middle of the night and knocks on your door and says: "We are late in arriving, but we have had trouble with our car, and here we are, and we have not had supper." You would go out to the refrigerator, and if you had even a little food there, which you could make to appear more by putting a little lettuce round it, you would serve that! You would not go in the middle of the night and knock on the door of your neighbor to borrow unless you had absolutely nothing. These three things are the principles of the human place in the ministry of the Word; love for souls, friendly communion with God, and that constant, utter and absolute acknowledgment of the fact that of ourselves we have nothing, and can have nothing. "A friend has come, and I have nothing." Thus we must turn to the Word of God. Any human message can be absolutely nothing unless the Lord shall speak, unless He shall take, and break, and use it to His glory.

The passage that will occupy our attention is one that speaks of beholding the Lord, and of being changed until our lives reflect His glory. And this transformation is the work of the indwelling Spirit. God is not in some far-off place; God dwells within those who have been born again. "Closer is He than

breathing, nearer than hands and feet." We need not
expect any blessing if we must look away to some far
distant God who is separated from us by great abysmal
distance. Christ has come to dwell within our hearts
through faith, and, though we see Him on the throne
of Heaven, yet He is with us in most intimate fellowship here on earth.

A great contrast is placed before us. We are to see in
the truths related to our text, illustration of the great
truth that is outlined doctrinally in the 8th of Romans.
"But we all, with open face beholding as in a glass the
glory of the Lord, are changed into the same image
from glory to glory, even as by the Spirit of the Lord."
This verse will illuminate the truth that Paul ex-
pounded in that chapter which stands as one of the
greatest in the Word: "For the law of the Spirit of life
in Christ Jesus hath made me free from the law of sin
and death. For what the law could not do in that it was
weak through the flesh, God, sending His own Son in
the likeness of sinful flesh, and for sin, condemned sin
in the flesh, that the righteousness of the law might be
fulfilled in us, who walk not after the flesh, but after
the Spirit" (Rom. 8:2–4).

The chapter in which our text is found is, in itself, a
great contrast. On the one hand, we have the giving of
the law described, with the emphasis laid on the glory
which surrounded Sinai and which filled the being of
Moses. On the other hand, we have the greater glory
of the ministration of the Holy Spirit of life in Christ
Jesus. Have you noticed how many times Paul speaks
of glory in this chapter? "The giving of the law was
glorious." The result was that Moses received a glory

upon his countenance. It is then stated that that was but a temporary glory, and that the giving of the Spirit was to be much more glorious. Then, lest some might have missed it, it is stated in terms of condemnation and righteousness. The giving of the one was attended with glory; it follows that a righteousness is greater than condemnation, so its glory is greater than the former. In fact that which was glorious can hardly be described as glory when compared with the greater glory which excelleth. Paul reverts to the phraseology of Romans. Again and again, he has contrasted the past with the present, using the term "much more" over and over again. Here he returns to this idea, saying: "For if that which is done away was glorious, much more that which remaineth is glorious." Thus, eleven times in a few brief verses he speaks of the glory of the giving of the law, and the greater glory that excels the former glory. Finally, our text uses the word glory yet three times more, telling us of the glory of the Lord, and promising that we shall be changed into the same image from glory to glory, even as by the Spirit of the Lord.

God has there put before us a tremendous contrast between the actual giving of the law and our position toward God in grace. From the Old Testament, He recalls the Mount of Sinai where He gave the law to Moses. He contrasts that occasion with the vision that is now ours through the living life of the Lord Jesus Christ dwelling within us.

There is a great body of matter concerning the Old Testament which is not found in it, but which is to be found in the New. A few years ago I began to note

in my Bible, information about the Old Testament
which is found in the New Testament but is not in the
Old Testament itself. There are many instances in
the New Testament where the Holy Spirit has given
an absolutely new revelation, where the Word of God
enlightens passages in the Old Testament which other-
wise we never would have fully understood. One of the
most striking examples is Enoch. We would not know
that Enoch had been translated, that he should not
see death, were it not for the New Testament. The
Old Testament merely tells us that Enoch walked with
God and he was not for God took him (Gen. 5:24). If
we had only had that verse, it might be claimed that
the phrase is a euphemism, a polite, pretty way of
saying that Enoch died. The New Testament tells us
that he did not die but was translated; that he should
not see death. It gives us further a paragraph out of
his sermon warning the ungodly of his day (Jude 14,
15). Similarly, in the passage in 2 Corinthians, the
narrative causes much wonder about an Old Testament event. Why were these things not told then, we
ask. We must realize, however, that God is giving a
fresh revelation of an old historical event in order to
emphasize the startling and striking difference so that
those in whose hearts the Holy Spirit dwells may
comprehend what is theirs in Him.

This change, this new knowledge in the New Testament, concerns the manner of the giving of the law.
One may remonstrate, "Was it not written in the
Old Testament that Moses told them to rope off a
space around Mount Sinai; that he went up; that he

saw God; that his face shone and that he had to put
a vail on his face?" That is true, but in the twelfth
chapter of Hebrews for instance, we read: "For ye
are not come unto the mount that might be touched,
and that burned with fire, nor unto blackness, and
darkness, and tempest, and the sound of a trumpet,
and the voice of words; which voice they that heard
entreated that the word should not be spoken to them
any more" (v. 18, 19). The Old Testament did not
record that when the law was being given the millions
of Israel cried out that they should not hear that voice
of God any more. "For they could not endure that
which was commanded, and if so much as a beast
touch the mountain, it shall be stoned, or thrust
through with a dart: and so terrible was the sight that
Moses said" (that which the Old Testament does not
mention), "I exceedingly fear and quake" (v. 20, 21).
Obviously, something happened there. But the passage
continues with a contrast: "But ye are come unto
Mount Sion, and unto the city of the living God, the
heavenly Jerusalem . . ." (v. 22).

The passage in 2nd Corinthians as well as this in
Hebrews offers a sharp contrast between two scenes.
In the book of Hebrews, two mountains are promi-
nent, Mount Sinai and Mount Sion—the law and
Calvary. In Corinthians, Paul is rather concerned
with the glory. At Sinai only one man got a message
from God, but now there is a power and a light for
every one of us who is in Christ Jesus. God is showing
that only by the coming of Christ, only by the ending
of the law, only by the beginning of grace, only

by the coming of the indwelling Spirit is it possible for any human being to have true righteousness within the heart.

The glory which now has come, the glory which excelleth, is a glory that makes alive. Its effect is to change us into the image of the Lord. We should remark just here, that many people say, in error, that man is made in the image of God. The truth is that Adam was created in the image of God, but that sin came and Adam died spiritually. The son which he begat was not in the image of God, but as the Scripture plainly declares, in his own fallen image. It is only when we are born again that the image of God "is renewed in knowledge after the image of Him that created him" (Col. 3:9, 10). That is how man can be made in the image of God. Other verses clearly teach the same truth. It is only as we pass from death into life in Christ that we are made safe in the image of God. Our text reveals how that image can be made to dominate within our lives.

The first point is that this glory is for every believer, not for the face of one man. Moses alone had the shining face at the giving of the law, but we all are to know the glory that is ours since Pentecost. In the day of grace, salvation and righteousness are not for a class, for a group, for a hierarchical overlordship, for priests who keep the people at an immeasurable distance below them. For in the sight of the Word of God there is no difference between the clergy and the laity. The fact that he may be spending his whole time in Christian work, studying the Word of God and giving forth the message, in no way puts a clergyman in a place apart. We are one in Christ Jesus. "I am the chief of sinners" (1 Tim. 1:15), said Paul, "less than the least of all the saints" (Eph. 3:8). Those who consider Paul the leader of them who give the message, see his own estimate of himself as he came directly in contact with the Word of God. Since no difference exists, we all can have that which God has given us through Christ.

We read in the 2nd chapter of the Acts of the Apostles that the blessing was not to be restricted. Your young men and your old men, your servants and your handmaidens, men and women, old and young, bond and free, sons and servants—all were to receive the Holy Spirit; in fact, He had come upon all. That is the word that was spoken and fulfilled at Pentecost. How different was that from what Moses heard when he saw the glory in the coming of the law. The people knew nothing of it; his was the only face that shone. All believers should know what it is to have the glory of that outshining light of the indwelling Holy Spirit.

The Lord Jesus Christ enunciates this same principle in a wonderful way in the Gospel of Matthew. You remember that John the Baptist when in prison became the prey of doubts, and sent his disciples to Jesus to question Him. After they had finished their errand and had left, Jesus, ever courteous, turned to the people in order to give them the proper view of John. The Lord said: "Verily, I say unto you, among them that are born of women there hath not risen a greater than John the Baptist" (Matt. 11:11). Stop and think what that means. Jesus is saying in effect:

"You may consider Moses, David, Solomon, Elijah, Elisha, Daniel, all the men of the Old Testament, but none of them have surpassed John the Baptist." This makes John the Baptist as great as any other Old Testament character, for he, of course, though found in the first pages of the Gospels, is the last of the Old Testament characters. Then Jesus adds this even more astounding word: "Notwithstanding, he that is least in the kingdom of Heaven is"—as great as? No—"greater than he!"

Now, if any man came before you today and said of himself: "I am greater than Moses, I am greater than Elijah, I am greater than Elisha, I am greater than Daniel, I am greater than all the heroes of the Old Testament," you would have every right to say: "What consummate egotism! What right has a man to speak like that?" But if any man should say: "I aspire to the title of the least in the kingdom of God," you would consider that he was speaking from his heart, and not from mock-humility, that he was not offending against modesty. Yet, to those who are least in the kingdom of God, the Lord says in effect: "In this age, since Pentecost, you are greater than John the Baptist," and therefore greater than all the men of the Old Testament. What truth this is! We heard the story the other day of a drunken wretch who had found the Lord Jesus Christ and had been transformed. The moment that the new birth had taken place it could be said of him that he was greater than Moses, greater than David, greater than Solomon, greater than John the Baptist. Why? Simply because of the greater glory that is now for us all.

We know, of course, that the passage refers primarily to those who shall be in the future kingdom, but it is none the less possible to apply this truth to the present age. We, as believers in the Lord Jesus Christ, have a higher standing than the saints of Old Testament times.

God has worked in three ways since the foundation of this world. Before Jesus Christ came, everything that was done may be summed up as done by God, *for* His people. Watch these prepositions. During the years when Jesus Christ was here His Name was Immanuel, which, being interpreted, is God *with* His people. But since the Day of Pentecost it is something far greater than that; it is God *in* His people. That is the reason why Jesus Christ was able to say that the least in the kingdom of Heaven is greater than John the Baptist. While the Spirit of God did come upon these men in a certain way for the inspiration of the Scriptures which they wrote, and for the work that they performed for God, they did not have the Holy Spirit dwelling within them, as you and I have Him dwelling within us. David indeed had been filled with the Spirit for his work, but in the 51st Psalm he prayed something which, thank God, you and I cannot pray: "Take not Thy Holy Spirit from me." For we have been sealed with the Holy Spirit until the day of redemption, and that is why the least today may be called greater than John the Baptist. Our God dwelleth in us. Our bodies are now the temples of the Holy Spirit. Let us not forget that. No place in this world has the right, Biblically speaking, to be called, in our day, a tabernacle or a temple. A church may be con-

secrated for the service of God, but even an abbey,
even a cathedral, even the mightiest ecclesiastical struc-
ture, at three o'clock in the morning, when it is empty,
is just as empty of the Holy Spirit of God as a tent.
On the other hand, the Spirit of God can meet you
there just as much as He can meet people where there
happen to be stained glass windows. Oh, thank God
for His grace! It is not for an inner circle! It is for you!
Every one of us may know that all that has been spoken
in the New Covenant is spoken for us.

Secondly, this vision of the Lord is to be ours
through the Word of God. Paul says: "We all, with
open face beholding as in a glass." There are many
symbols of the Bible to be found in the Bible itself.
It is the sword of the Spirit (Eph. 6:17). "Is not My
Word like . . . a hammer that breaketh the rock in
pieces?" (Jer. 23:29). It is like a fire: "Thy Word is a
lamp unto my feet, and a light unto my path" (Psa.
119:105). Paul speaks of it as a diet upon which we
feed; Hebrews 4:12 gives us still another word, though
the English "sword" in the Greek is "scalpel"; "The
Word of God is quick and powerful, and sharper than
any two-edged scalpel" (a surgeon's scalpel). James
calls it the seed of life: "Of His own will begat He us
with the Word of truth" (Jas. 1:18). The word in
Corinthians is but one more such example, for undoubtedly the glass is the Word of God. There it is
that we see the Lord Jesus Christ. He can be seen in no
other place today.

You are not going to find the Lord Jesus Christ
today in any ecstatic vision that comes by way of the
emotions. You are going to find Jesus Christ in the

Word of God, or you are not going to find Him. It is
important that we realize this. I suppose that every
Bible teacher has people coming to him from time to
time, saying: "I want to tell you about a vision I had."
Whenever anybody says that to me I say: "Now, wait
a moment. There was one man who had a vision, and
it was true, a God-given vision. He immediately said
that he saw things that were not lawful to be uttered,
and I would prefer that you did not utter your vision."
I am quite sure that if any of us really saw Jesus
Christ we should be like St. Paul, and say: "I saw
things beyond words, not lawful to be uttered." Today
is not the day of visions; today is the day of the
Word. This is our standard of judgment. If a man
comes to you and says: "Follow me. See, I have
worked miracles," do not for that reason follow him.
We must not forget that it is said that the working of
Satan is "with all power and signs and lying wonders."
God has given us His standard of judgment. "To the
law and to the testimony. If they speak not according
to this Word there is no light in them." "There are
three that bear witness in earth, the Spirit, and the
Word, and the blood; and these three agree in one."

Now that which is perfect is come. We have the
Word of God. That which is in part has been done
away and miracles are no longer the test for a man.
When a man speaks, those in the audience should be
measuring him by the Word of God, to determine
whether he is telling the truth by the Book. It was for
this last that Paul complimented the Bereans, for they
received the Word with all readiness of mind but
searched the Scriptures daily to see whether those

things were true (Acts 17:11). The Bereans would not
have believed something just because Paul taught it.
No man who loves the Lord and knows the Book in
any wise wishes that it should ever be said: "I believe
this because Dr. So-and-So teaches it." Oh, no, to
the law and to the testimony be the glory. We believe
because of the teaching of God's Word and test the
preaching of men by it.

Next, we are to notice that it is the glory of the Lord
Jesus Christ which we are to behold in His Word,
and the Holy Spirit will use the sight of this glory to
change us into the same image. The glory of the Lord
Jesus Christ is to be found throughout His Word. In
the year that King Uzziah died, Isaiah had his great
vision of the Lord, high and lifted up. You remember
that the seraphim cried: "Holy, holy, holy, is the Lord
of Hosts: the whole earth is full of His glory" (Isa. 6:3).
It was then that Isaiah saw his own worthlessness,
confessed his uncleanness, and was cleansed by the
touch of the coal on his lips from the altar. There is a
remarkable sidelight on this vision in the 12th chapter
of John's Gospel. Quoting from this very chapter in
Isaiah, John tells us: "These things said Isaiah when
he saw His glory and spake of Him." But whereas in
the prophecy of Isaiah the reference is clearly to the
glory of the Lord God of Hosts, in the Gospel the reference is clearly to the glory of the Lord Jesus Christ. The
inference is inescapable. The Lord Jesus occupied the
same place in the mind of John that Jehovah of Hosts
occupied in the mind of Isaiah. Things equal to the
same thing are equal to each other.

The outward manifestations of this glory were laid

aside when our Lord left the throne of Heaven to come to earth. It was of this that "He emptied Himself." The appurtenances of majesty remained in Heaven when He came in humility, but He was able to pray at the close of His life: "Glorify Thou Me with the glory I had with Thee before the world was" (John 17:5). And now He has gone to sit at the right hand of the Father, and this "God, who commanded the light to shine out of darkness, hath shined in our hearts, to give the light of the knowledge of the glory of God in the face of Jesus Christ" (2 Cor. 4:6). There is where we are told to behold it, and as we see it, others will see that we are indeed changed from glory to glory and will behold Him in us.

It is worth while remembering that no one will ever see in us that which we cannot see ourselves. The simple law of physics works in this spiritual matter. The angle of refraction is equal to the angle of incidence. But let me give you that in a story. My two small children came to my knees one day, and the smaller of the two was eagerly examining my features. Suddenly she said: "I see David in your eye." This surprised me, as I did not know you could see two images in an eye. I had often seen my own reflection in another eye, but I now realize the simple fact that the eye is a mirror. Anything that you can see yourself can be reflected from your eye. I took the boy and moved him, little by little, until I could see him no longer. As soon as I could not see him, the little girl said that she could not see him. Thus it is with our vision of the Lord. Keep Him in the center of your gaze, and all who look into your eye will see Him there.

Peter tells us in one of his epistles that God raised
Christ from the dead and gave Him glory. We are
not to confuse this glory with that for which Christ
prayed in the early part of His last great prayer. The
glory which He had with the Father before the world
was became His when He had completed His earthly
task. In addition to this, God gave Him a special
glory at the resurrection. It is of this last that Peter
speaks. And our Lord has taken care to leave us a
careful record of what He has done with that special
glory. "And the glory which Thou gavest Me, I have
given them" (John 17:22). He who endured the cross
for the joy that was set before Him, thought of us not
only in His death, but in the moment of His triumph.
The glory which He had so richly earned He set aside
for us. It is well for us to remember that we do not
have to wait until we reach Heaven in order to have
that glory. He wishes us to have it now. While the
Christian does not now have his glorified body, it is
none the less true that, beholding Him, we are changed
into the same image from glory to glory. There is no
place for drabness in the life that is yielded to Him.
Let us learn to know not only of the glory which shall
be, but of the glory which is the present possibility of
every life that is yielded to the working of the indwelling Spirit.

There is yet another point that is of great impor-
tance, and which must be stressed, especially in these
days. What does the Spirit mean when He tells us
"we are changed into the same image"? Here is the
true life-change. According to the Word of God, it
belongs only to Christians, only to those who have

been born again. You cannot change an unsaved man.
The old nature is condemned; God cannot do a thing
with it; God will not do a thing with it. He tells us
that the heart is deceitful above all things, and in-
curably sick. When God says a thing is incurable we
may well know that it is indeed incurable. All our
righteousnesses are as filthy rags in His sight. God does
not work with anything we have, with the thought of
changing it. There is always great danger that an
unsaved man will have some experience that is not
the new birth, but which will make him live a little
different life, so that he will say: "You see how
changed I am."

When I was in India I traveled along the famous
Great North Road that leads from Calcutta right
through the United Provinces and the Punjab to the
North-West Frontier. It was most interesting, of course,
to see all that was to be found in the villages through
which we passed, but the road itself interested me also.
At one side the road was just sand and dust for the
camels, as their soft feet cannot stand a hard road.
The main road, however, was the macadam highway
for motor cars. You can well imagine that in the rainy
season, when the camel road was a quagmire, it would
not be as easy walking there as on the paved road.
Suppose a man is making his way along the camel
road, up to his knees in the mud. Someone calls to
him to come over to the other side of the road. He
will have no difficulty in testifying that there has been
a great change. Now the broad road that leads to
destruction has a muddy side and a paved side. If
someone is walking on his way to destruction in the

foul mire of iniquity, and another comes along and shares the knowledge that there is a cleaner side, he may come over to a moral way of life and testify in turn: "My life has been changed; I have a changed life." Nevertheless, he would still be on the broad road leading to destruction, and would not have been born again. Reform, any moral change, is not sufficient. A *changed* life is *not* what the Bible teaches. The Bible teaches a *new* life, an *exchanged* life, not the changing of what already existed but the implanting of an absolutely new principle. That is the new birth which is from above. When we have received that new life which God gives, that living Presence grows and increases, changing everything in our lives so that the new nature dominates the old nature. We read in the second epistle to the Corinthians: "If any man be in Christ, he is a new creation" (5:17)—an absolutely new creation. But after we have been born again then comes the change. God plants the new life within, and then that new life is to take control.

It should be pointed out, too, that this change will have its effect in every phase of our life. If there is entire yieldedness to the work of the Spirit, there will be astonishing changes. We will have to learn that the Lord will come down paths in our lives which we have not used at all. He will lead us not merely into ways of sweetness and light, but into ways of boldness and courage for Himself.

I can illustrate that by this incident. Some time ago, just before I was leaving the States to go on a tour of the mission fields, I spoke one evening in one of the suburbs of New York. In introducing me, the chairman said: "I am going to ask Dr. Barnhouse to take a moment to tell us about his trip to the foreign mission fields." I explained that one of the reasons for my trip was to counteract a false impression that had been made shortly before. A commission had been sent out by a liberal group and had reported that all the missionaries were inferior people, and that they were not doing good work. Some of us believed that that report was false, and that it had no more value than the report of a group of color blind men who might be sent to study the paintings in the Louvre. How could these men, who were not stalwart defenders of the great doctrines of Scripture, bring back an adequate picture of what Christ is doing through missionaries in the foreign field? The next evening, in the same church, while the chairman was introducing me, an usher handed me a note. It was anonymous. I glanced at it and read: "Some of the listeners were deeply hurt last night when you spoke so harshly of Christian men by saying that they were color blind in their report on the missionaries. We hope that tonight you will display more of the spirit of the Master." If the letter had come to me at any other time it would not have been mentioned, but I took the occasion to say: "I want to ask the friends who wrote the letter and asked me to display the spirit of the Master: What phase of the spirit of the Master do they wish me to display? Do they wish me to say that these men are hypocrites, generation of vipers; that they are like graveyards, clean outside and full of dead men's bones within? Am I to say that they are filthy cups, with the outside clean?" That takes you aback, perhaps. Is that the spirit of the Master? Yes, that is the spirit of the Master, just as much as the fact that He was loving and kind, and went about doing good.

The Word of God tells us of our Lord Jesus Christ in Hebrews 1: "Thou hast loved righteousness and hated iniquity; therefore, God, even thy God, hath anointed thee with the oil of gladness above thy fellows" (v. 9). Therefore to be like Jesus must include a hatred of sin, just as much as it is to include a love of righteousness. The Holy Spirit will keep you careful that you do not turn that hatred toward individuals for the exaltation of your own pride. We must, as Paul puts it, "speak the truth in love." We must have the spirit of the Lord Jesus Christ upon us, changing us into His image. As you become more like Him you will hate everything that is mean, everything that is little, everything that is false. You will come to know Him better, and, as you become more like Him, you will find that He Himself is being reflected moment by moment in your life. I rather think, too, that those around you will see much more of the "going about doing good" than they will see of calling the enemy hypocrites. He will teach us the proper balance in all things.

The last clause brings us to our closing point. All this great and continuing transformation is to be "by the Spirit of the Lord." It is He who comes in to be the active and effective agent of all that God intends to do within us. In the measure that we yield to Him, He will do the glorious work. We need not expect that the change can take place in any other way. "What the law could not do in that it was weak through the flesh," God is going to do by "the law of the Spirit of life in Christ Jesus." That alone can "make us free from the law of sin and death." Frequently we are asked how it may be possible to cease walking after the flesh. God has given us a plain answer in the Galatian epistle. "This I say, Walk in the Spirit and ye shall not fulfil the lusts of the flesh" (5:16). It is simplicity itself. You cannot choose to put yourself in front of a fire on a cold day and still remain cold. The man who asks how he can cease walking after the flesh has a problem of the same nature as the man who would ask how he could stop being cold. There is a fire; go and stand before it, and the fire will do the work that is according to its nature. There is the Holy Spirit, planted within us, ready to do His warming, transforming work. Let Him take control. As naturally as fire banishes cold, He will bring glory into our life.

As we know Christ better, we come to know Him in different ways and by different names. When we first know Him, we think of Him as Jesus the Saviour. Later, we know Him as Lord and then a little farther along we come in the intimacy of our own thoughts to think of Him as the Rose of Sharon, the Altogether Lovely, the Beloved, the Fairest of Ten Thousand. With the natural reticence of our hearts and lives, we refrain from speaking of Him in the tenderest ways in public. Dr. Jowett has said that only Rutherford and Murray M'Cheyne, he thought, ever had the right to call the Lord, "Beloved," in public, because they had so lived with Him that the very love of Christ was stamped upon them and every one knew

that they lived with no other thoughts, no other
passions. In coming closer to Him, we learn more and
more of His Names and begin to enter into the Holy
of Holies, that wonderful inner chamber of communion with Him where we can say what He says to us:
"My Beloved is mine, and I am His" (S. of S. 2:16).

The teacher who dwells in the hearts, says: "Come,
see the Lord, come behold Him in the Word. Come
see in the glass the image of this One who, in the
vision of it, will be able to transform you from glory
to glory." Thus He speaks with us on the way.

When that wonderful girl of Ur of the Chaldees
was wooed by Eleazar for his absent master, Isaac,
she was told that she had to be ready to leave immediately to go back to Isaac. Her parents pled for ten
days' grace. Of what use they thought was such a
fine marriage if the wedding presents were not placed
on display that the other girls might see them! But
Eleazar said: "We must go." "Well," they said, "we
will ask the damsel." They asked her. She said: "I
will go." The young girl and the old man started on
that desert journey. What do you think they talked
about on the way? It doesn't say in the Word. Surely
young girls in those days were the same as they are
today and have been in all ages. Here was a young
girl on her way to be married to a young man she
never had seen. Can you not imagine her plying the
old man with persistent questions? "Tell me that
again, how tall did you say he is? What color are his
eyes? What is he like? Tell me that story about his
hunting? What else can you remember about him?"
All she wanted to hear as they went along on that

desert journey was more about Isaac. Day after day the slow, rolling motion of the camels marked the rhythm of her constant demand: "Tell me more of Isaac; tell me more of Isaac; tell me more of Isaac." Eleazar could talk of nothing else, but you may be sure that he originated the conversation. That was his design, that she might come to his master with a heart that should be filled with love because she had grown to know the one to whom she was going.

So it is with us. We are on our way to Him. The Holy Spirit, our Eleazar, goes with us, dwells within our hearts, speaks to us of Christ, and we all, beholding as in a glass the glory of the Lord, are changed into the same image from glory to glory, even by the Spirit of the Lord.